OGGIE TELLAM'S
BOOK OF CORNISH LIMERICKS

DAVID 'OGGIE' TELLAM

ACKNOWLEDGEMENTS

THE LIST of those to whom I owe thanks for encouragement is too extensive to mention here, but those to whom I owe special thanks are, Brian Tellam for the fine line drawings; Chris Moore for the water colouring of those drawings; Clive Baker for helping with the computer work; Jean Tellam for proof reading.

Oggie Tellam's Book of Cornish Limericks

© David 'Oggie' Tellam

First edition published 2006

Published by:
Palores Publishing
Redruth, Kernow

Printed by:
St Ives Printing & Publishing Company
High Street, St Ives, Cornwall TR26 1RS, UK

ISBN 0 9551878 1 8
ISBN 978 0 9551878 1 0

INTRODUCTION

I WAS once told by an aunt that I showed a very early disposition to rhyming speech.

She informed me that at the time when I was being weaned from the milk bottle; an elder brother, in the absence of my parents, filled an empty bottle with Guinness. He was, himself too young to be prosecuted for supplying alcohol to a minor — but he was duly chastised by our father when he discovered that a bottle of Guinness had gone missing from the crate, which he kept under his bed.

It was to late, the damage had been done.

Apparently, when the next feeding time came around I was said to scream:

"Dada, Mama, kiss-kiss, kiss-kiss!
Dada, Mama, Gin-giss, Gin-giss."

Thus began the original words of my limerick form.

DEDICATION

Dedicated to Councillor Roy Lobb.

A LEADING light who served the Parish of Chacewater for some thirty years and the District of Carrick for a quarter of a century.

Of many achievements he was instrumental in the establishment of Chacewater Health Centre, the Bowling Club, and the advanced status of Chacewater A.F.C.

He gave his all but took nothing.

Ny wra-ef vodya an bys-ma,
den bras y golon hep gormola.

Two gallant knights from Relubbus,
Looked to the stars, up above us.
They had lost their knights' charter,
So they said "Good King Arthur!
Will you please come back down and re-dub-us?"

5

A man on the beach in Portloe,
Looked up to the cliffs from below.
The tide was still rising;
With the dry land demising,
So, up the cliffs he decided to go.

There was a space man from Pendoggett,
Who arrived on the moon in his rocket.
Now the moonscape went bare,
So he said, "Since I'm here,
I will order new turfs and re-sod it."

A little boy called Owen from Crowan,
Had sow'en the seed of a Rowan,
Which sprouted and grew
As did the boy too,
Now they're both well and growing in Crowan.

A cat from Chacewater Cattery,
Was charged with assault and battery,
On a poor little bat,
That took a cat-nap,
On his way back home to the Battery.

A man rock climbing in Zennor,
Whose gear had cost him a tenner,
Had soon learned the ropes,
Then was scaling the slopes,
And he climbed there each day after dinner.

A Kangaroo from Pednavounder,
Who agreed to fight a 'three rounder',
Gave his 'oppo' a clout,
After the bell sounded out,
And was told, "You're a rotten young bounder!"

In Troon, the morn said "Goodbye!" to the moon.
"I look forward to seeing you soon.
I'll say farewell to the sun,
Just an hour before one;
Then I'm off for the whole afternoon."

In a drinking bowl down in Whitecross,
Were two water fleas swimming across.
When the dogs came to drink,
One flea said, "I think,
Our fate's in the lap of the dogs."

A punter who lives in St Day,
Places bets on the horses each way.
Though her looks are quite plain,
She plays well at the game,
And they say she can make a good lay.

A breeder of birds up in Summercourt,
Crossed a Pelican with a Grey Stork.
The result of his plan,
Was a type of Toucan;
And its Guinness they tinctured with Port.

Miss Green, a young lady from Crean,
Had gone for a swim in the stream.
A 'giant eel' appeared,
With a rusty red beard,
And frightened Miss Green, to ex-stream.

16

A young man walking through Reskadinnick,
Found a top and started to spin it.
When it started to sing,
The birds all joined in,
Led in song by a thronging cock linnet.

A miner who worked in Trenear,
Had quite a musical ear.
He used to work Poldark Mine,
But now spends his time,
Singing songs in the pub for his beer.

Two tinners who worked in Twelveheads,
Some spoil from the flume had just dredged.
They both had been planning,
To start on the vanning,
But decided on 'croust' time instead.

There was an old man from Townshend,
Who was given some watches to mend,
But was full of despair when,
He couldn't repair them.
He didn't know how much time he could spend.

A pigeon above Knave-Go-By,
Saw a Falcon to his right, way up high.
To his left was another,
The other one's brother;
Could they spy "Pigeon pie" in the sky?

A very thin man from Barripper,
Having drank a full barrel of bitter,
Dived into a pond,
Shouting, "I am James Bond!"
But he was only a drunk "skinny dipper."

A smart business girl from St Cleer,
Had taken to sell at the fair,
The choicest of fruits,
Some lovely beetroots,
And she also displayed a great pear.

A little girl by the name of Judy,
Who lived in a place called St Tudy,
With her dog known as Punch,
They'd each day after lunch,
Sit at the mirror and watch Punch and Judy.

An angler from Buryas Bridge,
Had baited his hook with a midge.
He then cast out the bait,
As it happened, too late:
Too much water passed under the bridge.

I once met a dog up in Pityme,
That jumped up and bit off a bit o' me.
So I bit the animal,
A black and white spaniel.
They say now that I'm its e-pit-o-me.

In Foxhole, a wiley old fox,
Who'd broken out in red spots,
Had caught many a fowl,
But started to howl,
When at last he had caught Chicken Pox.

There was an old man from Porkellis,
Who grew roses up on a trellis.
While his neighbour, Fred Friar,
Who grew only a briar,
Of the blooms, was exceedingly jealous.

There was an old man from New Mill.
Who, having completed his will,
Had tendered the reason,
I'm in life's last season,
And am rapidly going down hill.

There was a young fellow from Idless,
Who would drink nothing other than Guinness.
Now before they'd call time,
He would down twenty nine,
And be on his way home nearly legless.

A reluctant sailor, in fog off Torpoint,
Had his nose put right out of joint.
When his craft ran aground,
And he failed to go round,
Said, "I just couldn't see any point!"

A man up a ladder in Talskiddy,
Looked down to the ground and felt giddy.
It wasn't the height,
That caused him his plight,
He'd just drunk a large glass of 'Red Biddy.'

There was a young lady from Zelah,
Who went by the name of Miss Sheila.
Bad habits they say,
Have led her astray,
Since she's taken to drinking Tequila.

A short winded man from Warleggan,
Had entered a race to Pengegon.
When crossing the moors,
He developed foot sores,
But his chest is now cleared of the "Phleg'm."

That man who lives in St Ives,
Has been and divorced all his wives.
Now he's selling the cats,
Because all of the rats,
Have met with an early demise.

A high diver who lived in Trelash,
From a bank vault had stolen some cash.
He had hidden the hoard,
Up on the high board,
Now he's off for another big splash.

A surfer on Gwithian beach,
Had found himself way out of reach,
Of the shore and his safety,
But the life guards were hasty,
And threw him a line in the breach.

A man who sailed into St Mawes,
Claimed he'd seen a Great White just like Jaws.
Though he'd given his word,
He was told it's absurd,
And exposure to sun was the cause.

There was an old lady from Bugle,
Who had a pet poodle called Dougal;
That she fed a great deal
Of porridge oat meal.
But with the noodle and strudel, was frugal.

Michael McGoughan, a"Tar"from Bosoughan,
Brought home from the sea a pet Toucan.
Said his wife Ann-Marie,
"Now I'll have to feed three!
But can three live as cheaply as two can?"

In Perranwell was an old 'Wishing well',
Where an angler had thought of a spell.
He was granted his wish,
When he hooked a large fish,
Then declared, "What a swell fishing well!"

An old witch in her work shop in Trew,
Was busy with too much to do.
To reduce her work load,
She hired an old toad,
To help bottle the potions and brew.

An insect who lived in Lelant,
Went to visit his uncle in Kent.
But when he arrived,
He was very surprised,
For his uncle was really an Ant.

A donkey that lived in Nancledra,
Fell in love with a Jenny called Edna,
Who'd been made a curt 'pass,'
By a passing jackass;
But she bypassed them both for a zebra.

When valuing baked bread in Padstow,
The Judges in charge of the show,
Awarded cash prizes,
Depending on sizes,
That arose with the rise in the dough.

A police man patrolling in Gweek,
Had an "Angina" and felt very weak.
Now a bypass was tended,
And the heart duly mended,
Now they're both beating well on the beat.

An old mystic who lived in Loe Bar,
Had claimed that he owned a bright star.
At night it shone bright,
But by day out of sight,
When it's kept in an empty jam jar.

A ventriloquist who lived in Portreath,
Had stolen a large joint of beef.
He completely denied it,
But when asked who supplied it,
Told whopping great lies through his teeth.

A Banker who lived in Tresillian,
Fell asleep in the Cricket Pavilion.
There he spent pleasant dreams,
Counting bank notes in reams,
Which totalled, at least, half a million.

Cried a whaler when working Mounts Bay,
"There she blows! Let's set sail and make way!"
But the Calf and its "Mudder,"
Disconnected the rudder,
So no rudder, or blubber, that day.

A turtle who lived in Poundstock,
On its way to the Doc met a Crock.
"What's up?" said the Crock,
"You seem in a shock."
Said the turtle, "I'm just running amok."

A Cornish man from Penryn,
Had to mine hard rock to get tin.
While his daughter, Miss Porter,
In a stream at Chacewater,
Dipped a pan, and the tin, just streamed in.

An angler who fished off Porthoustock,
Told tales of great fish he had caught.
He was recalling a day,
When one got away,
And took with it the tackle and block.

There was a young witch from Polyphant,
Who travelled around on an elephant.
Just for transport, she seems,
To have gone to extremes;
But was granted the right by a 'Coven-aunt.'

A Game Keeper and his wife from Crowlas,
Had a marriage that was virtually rowless.
When emotions were raised,
They would go their own ways,
Scaring rooks until Crowlas was "Crowless."

A Saddler who worked in St Clether,
Made a lead from a long strip of leather.
When a goat was staked out,
It kept ranting about,
But soon came to the end of its tether.

The Countess of Constantine,
For the Count was beginning to pine.
Since he left in October,
She has never been sober,
And the cellar's now empty of wine.

A weight lifter from Camborne West,
Was benching well below best,
When a quote in the Mirror,
Claimed he'd made a bad error,
But did he just have one bad press?

A gardener who lived in Penryn,
Had some trees that he needed to trim.
He slipped on a branch,
Lost his sense of balance,
And then found himself out on a limb.

A psychiatrist who practiced near Trink,
Walking home from the pub full of drink,
Had his cloak and cap donned,
But they're now in the pond.
Will the "shrink" full of drink float or sink?

There was a young athlete from Wendron,
Who injured his Ach-ill-es tendon.
The tension was eased,
When he wrapped it in leaves,
That he picked from a wild rhododendron.

By the water side down in Flushing,
Sat a maid with red hair who was blushing.
The reason you see,
A young man from the sea,
Had an effect on her, truly, most crushing.

There was a young man from Carn Brea,
Who went into the castle to stay,
He was awoken one night,
By the ghost of a knight;
When his shock of black hair turned to grey.

There was a young man from New Mill,
Who was always seeking a thrill.
He stole a new Porsche,
Then ran into a horse,
But he's not thrilled, being grilled, by the Bill.

An old Celt from Castle-an-dinas,
Had sons called Linny and Linus.
Now Linny was tall,
But Linus was small,
And measured some six inches minus.

An old woman from Mylor Bridge,
Used to keep her pet mice in a fridge.
They absconded one day,
With a clean getaway,
Up the drainpipe and over the ridge.

A parrot that lived in Mount Hawke,
Was barely able to squawk.
But he was no fool,
So he went to night school,
And now he's able to talk.

There lives a strange man in St Ives,
Whose appearance his shrewdness belies,
For he goes dressed like a tramp,
And looks grossly unkempt,
But can converse with the witless or wise.